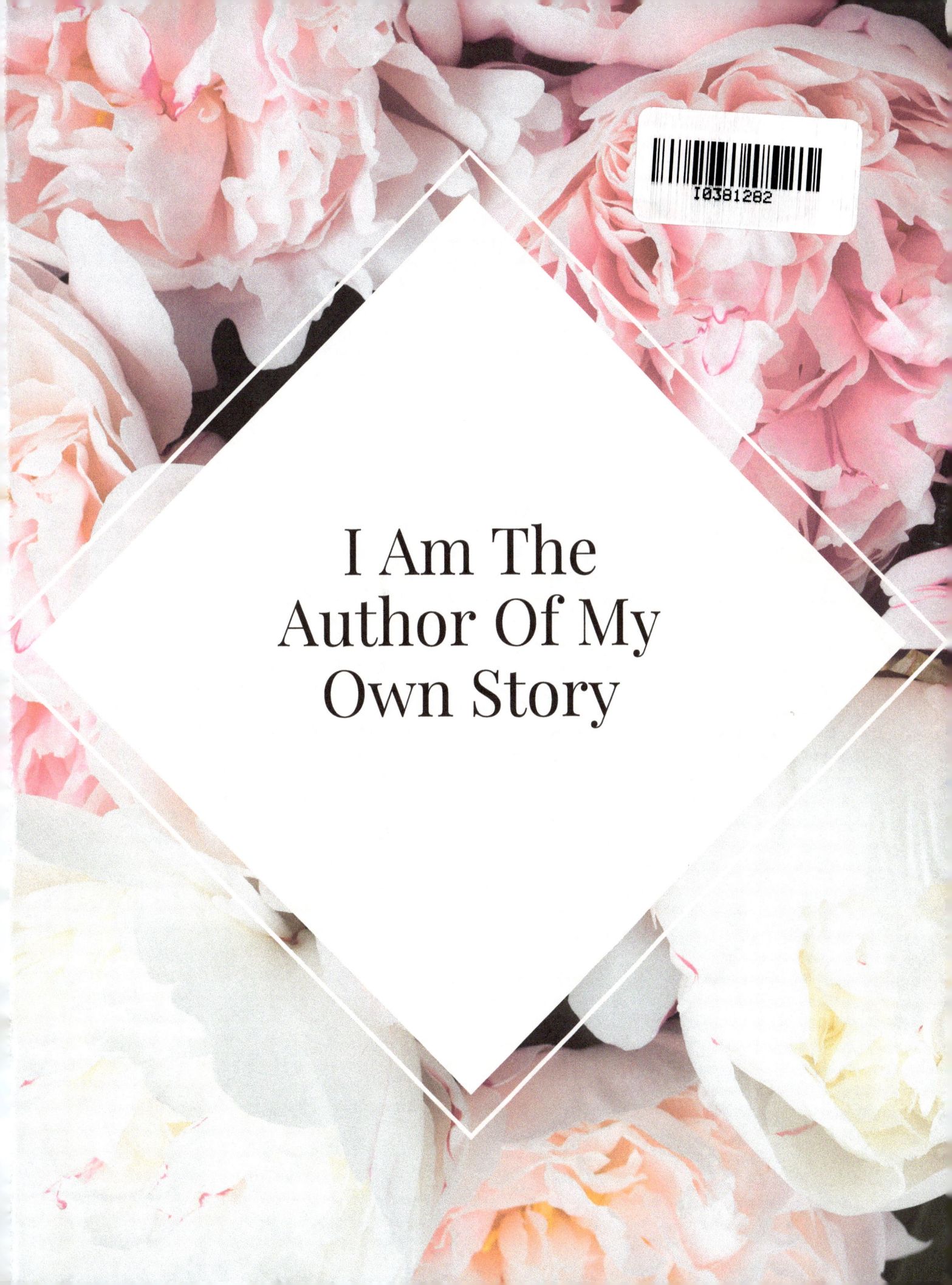

I Am The Author Of My Own Story

30-Days of Gratitude

This journal is a guide for beginning the rest of your journey into mastering manifestations via the Law of Attraction. It includes positive prompts, inspirational quotes and statements for a full 30 days of gratitude.

Journaling allows you to clearly set goals and visualize your desired life, while establishing positive thinking habits and allowing time for reflection. The Law of Attraction means you are in control of what you attract. You are in control of what you manifest.

Use Gratitude to harness the power within:

Ask, believe, and receive.

30 DAYS OF GRATITUDE

MONDAY	TUESDAY	WEDNESDAY	THURSDAY	FRIDAY	SATURDAY	SUNDAY
☐	☐	☐	☐	☐	☐	☐
☐	☐	☐	☐	☐	☐	☐
☐	☐	☐	☐	☐	☐	☐
☐	☐	☐	☐	☐	☐	☐
☐	☐	☐	☐	☐	☐	☐

21-DAY HABITS TRACKER

HABITS	1	2	3	4	5	6	7	8	9	10	11	12	13	14	15	16	17	18	19	20	21

STRUGGLES WITH KEEPING HABITS

HOW DID I SUCCEED?

DAY 1

- Select any affirmation and repeat it 5 times.
- Recall and repeat this mantra throughout the day.
- Harness positive energy via 15 - 20 minutes of meditation.
- Visualize the life you desire.

List 10 things you are *grateful* for today.

DAILY POSITIVITY

Today is:

I Woke Up At:

Month 1   2   3   4   5   6   7   8   9   10   11   12   Year
       Jan Feb Mar Apr May Jun Jul Aug Sep Oct Nov Dec

TODAY'S GOAL

THREE THINGS I'M GRATEFUL

THREE ACTS OF KINDNESS

TASKS

- ◯
- ◯
- ◯
- ◯
- ◯
- ◯
- ◯
- ◯
- ◯
- ◯
- ◯
- ◯
- ◯
- ◯
- ◯
- ◯
- ◯
- ◯

TODAY'S CHALLENGES

THE BEST THING ABOUT TODAY

GOLDEN OPPORTUNITIES

NOTES

DAY 2

- Select any affirmation and repeat it 5 times.
- Recall and repeat this mantra throughout the day.
- Harness positive energy via 15 - 20 minutes of meditation.
- Visualize the life you desire.

 **Who are you most grateful for in your life today? Why?**

DAILY POSITIVITY

Today is:

I Woke Up At:

| Month | 1 Jan | 2 Feb | 3 Mar | 4 Apr | 5 May | 6 Jun | 7 Jul | 8 Aug | 9 Sep | 10 Oct | 11 Nov | 12 Dec | Year |

TODAY'S GOAL

THREE THINGS I'M GRATEFUL

THREE ACTS OF KINDNESS

TASKS

○
○
○
○
○
○
○
○
○
○
○
○
○
○
○
○

TODAY'S CHALLENGES

THE BEST THING ABOUT TODAY

GOLDEN OPPORTUNITIES

NOTES

DAY 3

- Select any affirmation and repeat it 5 times.
- Recall and repeat this mantra throughout the day.
- Harness positive energy via 15 - 20 minutes of meditation.
- Visualize the life you desire.

 **What skills and traits are you most thankful to have?**

DAILY POSITIVITY

Today is:

I Woke Up At:

Month 1   2   3   4   5   6   7   8   9   10   11   12   Year
       Jan Feb Mar Apr May Jun Jul Aug Sep Oct Nov Dec

TODAY'S GOAL

THREE THINGS I'M GRATEFUL

THREE ACTS OF KINDNESS

TASKS

○
○
○
○
○
○
○
○
○
○
○
○
○
○
○
○

TODAY'S CHALLENGES

THE BEST THING ABOUT TODAY

GOLDEN OPPORTUNITIES

NOTES

DAY 4

- Select any affirmation and repeat it 5 times.
- Recall and repeat this mantra throughout the day.
- Harness positive energy via 15 - 20 minutes of meditation.
- Visualize the life you desire.

 **Recall a recent hardship – how did you learn from it?**

DAILY POSITIVITY

Today is: I Woke Up At:

Month   1   2   3   4   5   6   7   8   9   10   11   12   Year
        Jan   Feb   Mar   Apr   May   Jun   Jul   Aug   Sep   Oct   Nov   Dec

TODAY'S GOAL

THREE THINGS I'M GRATEFUL

THREE ACTS OF KINDNESS

TASKS

- ○
- ○
- ○
- ○
- ○
- ○
- ○
- ○
- ○
- ○
- ○
- ○
- ○
- ○
- ○
- ○
- ○

TODAY'S CHALLENGES

THE BEST THING ABOUT TODAY

GOLDEN OPPORTUNITIES

NOTES

DAY 5

- Select any affirmation and repeat it 5 times.
- Recall and repeat this mantra throughout the day.
- Harness positive energy via 15 - 20 minutes of meditation.
- Visualize the life you desire.

 **What simple part of your life are you most grateful for?**

DAILY POSITIVITY

Today is: I Woke Up At:

Month   1   2   3   4   5   6   7   8   9   10   11   12   Year
        Jan   Feb   Mar   Apr   May   Jun   Jul   Aug   Sep   Oct   Nov   Dec

TODAY'S GOAL

THREE THINGS I'M GRATEFUL

THREE ACTS OF KINDNESS

TASKS

- ○
- ○
- ○
- ○
- ○
- ○
- ○
- ○
- ○
- ○
- ○
- ○
- ○
- ○
- ○
- ○
- ○

TODAY'S CHALLENGES

THE BEST THING ABOUT TODAY

GOLDEN OPPORTUNITIES

NOTES

DAY 6

- Select any affirmation and repeat it 5 times.
- Recall and repeat this mantra throughout the day.
- Harness positive energy via 15 - 20 minutes of meditation.
- Visualize the life you desire.

 Who had done something to help or make your life easier?

DAILY POSITIVITY

Today is:

I Woke Up At:

| Month | 1 Jan | 2 Feb | 3 Mar | 4 Apr | 5 May | 6 Jun | 7 Jul | 8 Aug | 9 Sep | 10 Oct | 11 Nov | 12 Dec | Year |

TODAY'S GOAL

THREE THINGS I'M GRATEFUL

THREE ACTS OF KINDNESS

TASKS

-
-
-
-
-
-
-
-
-
-
-
-
-
-
-
-

TODAY'S CHALLENGES

THE BEST THING ABOUT TODAY

GOLDEN OPPORTUNITIES

NOTES

DAY 7

- Select any affirmation and repeat it 5 times.
- Recall and repeat this mantra throughout the day.
- Harness positive energy via 15 - 20 minutes of meditation.
- Visualize the life you desire.

 **Which part or parts of nature are you most grateful for?**

DAILY POSITIVITY

Today is:

I Woke Up At:

Month 1   2   3   4   5   6   7   8   9   10   11   12   Year
       Jan Feb Mar Apr May Jun Jul Aug Sep Oct Nov Dec

TODAY'S GOAL

THREE THINGS I'M GRATEFUL

THREE ACTS OF KINDNESS

TASKS

○
○
○
○
○
○
○
○
○
○
○
○
○
○
○
○
○

TODAY'S CHALLENGES

THE BEST THING ABOUT TODAY

GOLDEN OPPORTUNITIES

NOTES

LIST OF THINGS
I AM THANKFUL FOR THIS WEEK

WEEK

MONDAY

TUESDAY

WEDNESDAY

THURSDAY

FRIDAY

SATURDAY

SUNDAY

WEEKLY REVIEW

WEEK

| MONDAY | TUESDAY | WEDNESDAY |

| THURSDAY | FRIDAY |

| SATURDAY | SUNDAY |

A SUMMARY OF THE WHOLE WEEK

DAY 8

- Select any affirmation and repeat it 5 times.
- Recall and repeat this mantra throughout the day.
- Harness positive energy via 15 - 20 minutes of meditation.
- Visualize the life you desire.

 **List 10 materials you are most gratful for.**

DAILY POSITIVITY

Today is: I Woke Up At:

Month   1   2   3   4   5   6   7   8   9   10   11   12   Year
          Jan   Feb   Mar   Apr   May   Jun   Jul   Aug   Sep   Oct   Nov   Dec

TODAY'S GOAL

THREE THINGS I'M GRATEFUL

THREE ACTS OF KINDNESS

TASKS

- ○
- ○
- ○
- ○
- ○
- ○
- ○
- ○
- ○
- ○
- ○
- ○
- ○
- ○
- ○
- ○
- ○

TODAY'S CHALLENGES

THE BEST THING ABOUT TODAY

GOLDEN OPPORTUNITIES

NOTES

DAY 9

- Select any affirmation and repeat it 5 times.
- Recall and repeat this mantra throughout the day.
- Harness positive energy via 15 - 20 minutes of meditation.
- Visualize the life you desire.

 Write a thank you to the most influential person in your life – past or present.

DAILY POSITIVITY

Today is:

I Woke Up At:

Month	1	2	3	4	5	6	7	8	9	10	11	12	Year
	Jan	Feb	Mar	Apr	May	Jun	Jul	Aug	Sep	Oct	Nov	Dec	

TODAY'S GOAL

THREE THINGS I'M GRATEFUL

THREE ACTS OF KINDNESS

TASKS

- ○
- ○
- ○
- ○
- ○
- ○
- ○
- ○
- ○
- ○
- ○
- ○
- ○
- ○
- ○
- ○
- ○

TODAY'S CHALLENGES

THE BEST THING ABOUT TODAY

GOLDEN OPPORTUNITIES

NOTES

DAY 10

- Select any affirmation and repeat it 5 times.
- Recall and repeat this mantra throughout the day.
- Harness positive energy via 15 - 20 minutes of meditation.
- Visualize the life you desire.

 Think back to where you were 5 years ago. What life changes are you most grateful for?

DAILY POSITIVITY

Today is: | I Woke Up At:

Month 1   2   3   4   5   6   7   8   9   10   11   12   Year
       Jan Feb Mar Apr May Jun Jul Aug Sep Oct Nov Dec

TODAY'S GOAL

THREE THINGS I'M GRATEFUL

THREE ACTS OF KINDNESS

TASKS

○
○
○
○
○
○
○
○
○
○
○
○
○
○
○
○
○

TODAY'S CHALLENGES

THE BEST THING ABOUT TODAY

GOLDEN OPPORTUNITIES

NOTES

DAY 11

- Select any affirmation and repeat it 5 times.
- Recall and repeat this mantra throughout the day.
- Harness positive energy via 15 - 20 minutes of meditation.
- Visualize the life you desire.

 **Which foods or beverage are you most grateful for?**

DAILY POSITIVITY

Today is:

I Woke Up At:

Month	1	2	3	4	5	6	7	8	9	10	11	12	Year
	Jan	Feb	Mar	Apr	May	Jun	Jul	Aug	Sep	Oct	Nov	Dec	

TODAY'S GOAL

THREE THINGS I'M GRATEFUL

THREE ACTS OF KINDNESS

TASKS

- ○
- ○
- ○
- ○
- ○
- ○
- ○
- ○
- ○
- ○
- ○
- ○
- ○
- ○
- ○
- ○
- ○

TODAY'S CHALLENGES

THE BEST THING ABOUT TODAY

GOLDEN OPPORTUNITIES

NOTES

DAY 12

- Select any affirmation and repeat it 5 times.
- Recall and repeat this mantra throughout the day.
- Harness positive energy via 15 - 20 minutes of meditation.
- Visualize the life you desire.

 **What can you do to show someone you are grateful for them?**

DAILY POSITIVITY

Today is: _____   I Woke Up At: _____

Month 1   2   3   4   5   6   7   8   9   10   11   12   Year
       Jan Feb Mar Apr May Jun Jul Aug Sep Oct Nov Dec

TODAY'S GOAL

THREE THINGS I'M GRATEFUL

THREE ACTS OF KINDNESS

TASKS

- ○
- ○
- ○
- ○
- ○
- ○
- ○
- ○
- ○
- ○
- ○
- ○
- ○
- ○
- ○
- ○
- ○
- ○

TODAY'S CHALLENGES

THE BEST THING ABOUT TODAY

GOLDEN OPPORTUNITIES

NOTES

DAY 13

- Select any affirmation and repeat it 5 times.
- Recall and repeat this mantra throughout the day.
- Harness positive energy via 15 - 20 minutes of meditation.
- Visualize the life you desire.

Oprah Winfrey once said:

"Be thankful for what you have; you'll end up having more. If you concentrate on what you don't have, you will never, ever have enough."

Do you agree? Why, or why not?

DAILY POSITIVITY

Today is: _____   I Woke Up At: _____

Month 1   2   3   4   5   6   7   8   9   10   11   12   Year
       Jan   Feb   Mar   Apr   May   Jun   Jul   Aug   Sep   Oct   Nov   Dec

TODAY'S GOAL

THREE THINGS I'M GRATEFUL

THREE ACTS OF KINDNESS

TASKS

- ○
- ○
- ○
- ○
- ○
- ○
- ○
- ○
- ○
- ○
- ○
- ○
- ○
- ○
- ○
- ○
- ○

TODAY'S CHALLENGES

THE BEST THING ABOUT TODAY

GOLDEN OPPORTUNITIES

NOTES

DAY 14

- Select any affirmation and repeat it 5 times.
- Recall and repeat this mantra throughout the day.
- Harness positive energy via 15 - 20 minutes of meditation.
- Visualize the life you desire.

 **What accomplishments have brought you the most joy and fulfillment?**

DAILY POSITIVITY

Today is: I Woke Up At:

| Month | 1 Jan | 2 Feb | 3 Mar | 4 Apr | 5 May | 6 Jun | 7 Jul | 8 Aug | 9 Sep | 10 Oct | 11 Nov | 12 Dec | Year |

TODAY'S GOAL

THREE THINGS I'M GRATEFUL

THREE ACTS OF KINDNESS

TASKS

- ○
- ○
- ○
- ○
- ○
- ○
- ○
- ○
- ○
- ○
- ○
- ○
- ○
- ○
- ○
- ○
- ○

TODAY'S CHALLENGES

THE BEST THING ABOUT TODAY

GOLDEN OPPORTUNITIES

NOTES

LIST OF THINGS
I AM THANKFUL FOR THIS WEEK

WEEK

MONDAY

TUESDAY

WEDNESDAY

THURSDAY

FRIDAY

SATURDAY

SUNDAY

WEEKLY REVIEW

WEEK

| MONDAY | TUESDAY | WEDNESDAY |

| THURSDAY | FRIDAY |

| SATURDAY | SUNDAY |

A SUMMARY OF THE WHOLE WEEK

DAY 15

- Select any affirmation and repeat it 5 times.
- Recall and repeat this mantra throughout the day.
- Harness positive energy via 15 - 20 minutes of meditation.
- Visualize the life you desire.

 **How difficult would your life be without your closest loved one?**

DAILY POSITIVITY

Today is:

I Woke Up At:

Month 1   2   3   4   5   6   7   8   9   10   11   12   Year
       Jan Feb Mar Apr May Jun Jul Aug Sep Oct Nov Dec

TODAY'S GOAL

THREE THINGS I'M GRATEFUL

THREE ACTS OF KINDNESS

TASKS

- ○
- ○
- ○
- ○
- ○
- ○
- ○
- ○
- ○
- ○
- ○
- ○
- ○
- ○
- ○
- ○
- ○
- ○

TODAY'S CHALLENGES

THE BEST THING ABOUT TODAY

GOLDEN OPPORTUNITIES

NOTES

DAY 16

- Select any affirmation and repeat it 5 times.
- Recall and repeat this mantra throughout the day.
- Harness positive energy via 15 - 20 minutes of meditation.
- Visualize the life you desire.

 What was the last act of kindness you did? Think of ways you can make 5 strangers smile tomorrow.

DAILY POSITIVITY

Today is: I Woke Up At:

| Month | 1 Jan | 2 Feb | 3 Mar | 4 Apr | 5 May | 6 Jun | 7 Jul | 8 Aug | 9 Sep | 10 Oct | 11 Nov | 12 Dec | Year |

TODAY'S GOAL

THREE THINGS I'M GRATEFUL

THREE ACTS OF KINDNESS

TASKS

- ○
- ○
- ○
- ○
- ○
- ○
- ○
- ○
- ○
- ○
- ○
- ○
- ○
- ○
- ○
- ○
- ○
- ○

TODAY'S CHALLENGES

THE BEST THING ABOUT TODAY

GOLDEN OPPORTUNITIES

NOTES

DAY 17

- Select any affirmation and repeat it 5 times.
- Recall and repeat this mantra throughout the day.
- Harness positive energy via 15 - 20 minutes of meditation.
- Visualize the life you desire.

 What is your favorite family tradition? Share what you like most about it.

DAILY POSITIVITY

Today is:

I Woke Up At:

| Month | 1 Jan | 2 Feb | 3 Mar | 4 Apr | 5 May | 6 Jun | 7 Jul | 8 Aug | 9 Sep | 10 Oct | 11 Nov | 12 Dec | Year |

TODAY'S GOAL

THREE THINGS I'M GRATEFUL

THREE ACTS OF KINDNESS

TASKS

- ○
- ○
- ○
- ○
- ○
- ○
- ○
- ○
- ○
- ○
- ○
- ○
- ○
- ○
- ○
- ○
- ○

TODAY'S CHALLENGES

THE BEST THING ABOUT TODAY

GOLDEN OPPORTUNITIES

NOTES

DAY 18

- Select any affirmation and repeat it 5 times.
- Recall and repeat this mantra throughout the day.
- Harness positive energy via 15 - 20 minutes of meditation.
- Visualize the life you desire.

 What made you smile today? What made you laugh?

DAILY POSITIVITY

Today is: I Woke Up At:

Month 1   2   3   4   5   6   7   8   9   10   11   12   Year
       Jan Feb Mar Apr May Jun Jul Aug Sep Oct Nov Dec

TODAY'S GOAL

THREE THINGS I'M GRATEFUL

THREE ACTS OF KINDNESS

TASKS

-
-
-
-
-
-
-
-
-
-
-
-
-
-
-
-
-

TODAY'S CHALLENGES

THE BEST THING ABOUT TODAY

GOLDEN OPPORTUNITIES

NOTES

DAY 19

- Select any affirmation and repeat it 5 times.
- Recall and repeat this mantra throughout the day.
- Harness positive energy via 15 - 20 minutes of meditation.
- Visualize the life you desire.

 **Describe your ideal Sunday. How can you make today feel more like that perfect day?**

DAILY POSITIVITY

Today is:

I Woke Up At:

Month 1   2   3   4   5   6   7   8   9   10 11 12 Year
       Jan Feb Mar Apr May Jun Jul Aug Sep Oct Nov Dec

TODAY'S GOAL

THREE THINGS I'M GRATEFUL

THREE ACTS OF KINDNESS

TASKS

- ○
- ○
- ○
- ○
- ○
- ○
- ○
- ○
- ○
- ○
- ○
- ○
- ○
- ○
- ○
- ○
- ○

TODAY'S CHALLENGES

THE BEST THING ABOUT TODAY

GOLDEN OPPORTUNITIES

NOTES

DAY 20

- Select any affirmation and repeat it 5 times.
- Recall and repeat this mantra throughout the day.
- Harness positive energy via 15 - 20 minutes of meditation.
- Visualize the life you desire.

 **JOHN F. KENNEDY ONCE SAID:**

"As we express our gratitude, we must never forget that the highest appreciation is not to utter words, but to live by them"

Do you agree? Why, or why not?

DAILY POSITIVITY

Today is: I Woke Up At:

| Month | 1 Jan | 2 Feb | 3 Mar | 4 Apr | 5 May | 6 Jun | 7 Jul | 8 Aug | 9 Sep | 10 Oct | 11 Nov | 12 Dec | Year |

TODAY'S GOAL

THREE THINGS I'M GRATEFUL

THREE ACTS OF KINDNESS

TASKS

- ○
- ○
- ○
- ○
- ○
- ○
- ○
- ○
- ○
- ○
- ○
- ○
- ○
- ○
- ○
- ○
- ○

TODAY'S CHALLENGES

THE BEST THING ABOUT TODAY

GOLDEN OPPORTUNITIES

NOTES

DAY 21

- Select any affirmation and repeat it 5 times.
- Recall and repeat this mantra throughout the day.
- Harness positive energy via 15 - 20 minutes of meditation.
- Visualize the life you desire.

What is one of "the little things" you think is most under appreciated? why?

DAILY POSITIVITY

Today is:

I Woke Up At:

Month	1	2	3	4	5	6	7	8	9	10	11	12	Year
	Jan	Feb	Mar	Apr	May	Jun	Jul	Aug	Sep	Oct	Nov	Dec	

TODAY'S GOAL

THREE THINGS I'M GRATEFUL

THREE ACTS OF KINDNESS

TASKS

- ○
- ○
- ○
- ○
- ○
- ○
- ○
- ○
- ○
- ○
- ○
- ○
- ○
- ○
- ○
- ○
- ○
- ○

TODAY'S CHALLENGES

THE BEST THING ABOUT TODAY

GOLDEN OPPORTUNITIES

NOTES

LIST OF THINGS
I AM THANKFUL FOR THIS WEEK

WEEK

MONDAY

TUESDAY

WEDNESDAY

THURSDAY

FRIDAY

SATURDAY

SUNDAY

WEEKLY REVIEW

WEEK

MONDAY

TUESDAY

WEDNESDAY

THURSDAY

FRIDAY

SATURDAY

SUNDAY

A SUMMARY OF THE WHOLE WEEK

DAY 22

- Select any affirmation and repeat it 5 times.
- Recall and repeat this mantra throughout the day.
- Harness positive energy via 15 - 20 minutes of meditation.
- Visualize the life you desire.

 Being thankful is the best thing you can possibly be. Do you agree or disagree?

DAILY POSITIVITY

Today is:

I Woke Up At:

Month 1   2   3   4   5   6   7   8   9   10   11   12   Year
       Jan Feb Mar Apr May Jun Jul Aug Sep Oct Nov Dec

TODAY'S GOAL

THREE THINGS I'M GRATEFUL

THREE ACTS OF KINDNESS

TASKS

- ○
- ○
- ○
- ○
- ○
- ○
- ○
- ○
- ○
- ○
- ○
- ○
- ○
- ○
- ○
- ○
- ○

TODAY'S CHALLENGES

THE BEST THING ABOUT TODAY

GOLDEN OPPORTUNITIES

NOTES

DAY 23

- Select any affirmation and repeat it 5 times.
- Recall and repeat this mantra throughout the day.
- Harness positive energy via 15 - 20 minutes of meditation.
- Visualize the life you desire.

 Reflect on your favorite childhood memory. What made it so great?

DAILY POSITIVITY

Today is:

I Woke Up At:

Month	1	2	3	4	5	6	7	8	9	10	11	12	Year
	Jan	Feb	Mar	Apr	May	Jun	Jul	Aug	Sep	Oct	Nov	Dec	

TODAY'S GOAL

THREE THINGS I'M GRATEFUL

THREE ACTS OF KINDNESS

TASKS

- ○
- ○
- ○
- ○
- ○
- ○
- ○
- ○
- ○
- ○
- ○
- ○
- ○
- ○
- ○
- ○
- ○

TODAY'S CHALLENGES

THE BEST THING ABOUT TODAY

GOLDEN OPPORTUNITIES

NOTES

DAY 24

- Select any affirmation and repeat it 5 times.
- Recall and repeat this mantra throughout the day.
- Harness positive energy via 15 - 20 minutes of meditation.
- Visualize the life you desire.

 What was something beautiful or striking you saw today?

DAILY POSITIVITY

Today is:

I Woke Up At:

| Month | 1 Jan | 2 Feb | 3 Mar | 4 Apr | 5 May | 6 Jun | 7 Jul | 8 Aug | 9 Sep | 10 Oct | 11 Nov | 12 Dec | Year |

TODAY'S GOAL

THREE THINGS I'M GRATEFUL

THREE ACTS OF KINDNESS

TASKS

- ○
- ○
- ○
- ○
- ○
- ○
- ○
- ○
- ○
- ○
- ○
- ○
- ○
- ○
- ○
- ○
- ○
- ○

TODAY'S CHALLENGES

THE BEST THING ABOUT TODAY

GOLDEN OPPORTUNITIES

NOTES

DAY 25

- Select any affirmation and repeat it 5 times.
- Recall and repeat this mantra throughout the day.
- Harness positive energy via 15 - 20 minutes of meditation.
- Visualize the life you desire.

 What would you tell your best friend that you like most about them?

DAILY POSITIVITY

Today is:

I Woke Up At:

Month	1	2	3	4	5	6	7	8	9	10	11	12	Year
	Jan	Feb	Mar	Apr	May	Jun	Jul	Aug	Sep	Oct	Nov	Dec	

TODAY'S GOAL

THREE THINGS I'M GRATEFUL

THREE ACTS OF KINDNESS

TASKS

- ○
- ○
- ○
- ○
- ○
- ○
- ○
- ○
- ○
- ○
- ○
- ○
- ○
- ○
- ○
- ○
- ○

TODAY'S CHALLENGES

THE BEST THING ABOUT TODAY

GOLDEN OPPORTUNITIES

NOTES

DAY 26

- Select any affirmation and repeat it 5 times.
- Recall and repeat this mantra throughout the day.
- Harness positive energy via 15 - 20 minutes of meditation.
- Visualize the life you desire.

 What is your favorite quote about gratitude? Why does it resonate with you?

DAILY POSITIVITY

Today is:

I Woke Up At:

Month 1   2   3   4   5   6   7   8   9   10 11 12 Year
       Jan Feb Mar Apr May Jun Jul Aug Sep Oct Nov Dec

TODAY'S GOAL

THREE THINGS I'M GRATEFUL

THREE ACTS OF KINDNESS

TASKS

- ○
- ○
- ○
- ○
- ○
- ○
- ○
- ○
- ○
- ○
- ○
- ○
- ○
- ○
- ○
- ○
- ○
- ○

TODAY'S CHALLENGES

THE BEST THING ABOUT TODAY

GOLDEN OPPORTUNITIES

NOTES

DAY 27

- Select any affirmation and repeat it 5 times.
- Recall and repeat this mantra throughout the day.
- Harness positive energy via 15 - 20 minutes of meditation.
- Visualize the life you desire.

 What is an embarrassing thing you are most grateful never happened?

DAILY POSITIVITY

Today is: I Woke Up At:

Month 1   2   3   4   5   6   7   8   9   10   11   12   Year
       Jan Feb Mar Apr May Jun Jul Aug Sep Oct Nov Dec

TODAY'S GOAL

THREE THINGS I'M GRATEFUL

THREE ACTS OF KINDNESS

TASKS

- ○
- ○
- ○
- ○
- ○
- ○
- ○
- ○
- ○
- ○
- ○
- ○
- ○
- ○
- ○
- ○
- ○

TODAY'S CHALLENGES

THE BEST THING ABOUT TODAY

GOLDEN OPPORTUNITIES

NOTES

DAY 28

- Select any affirmation and repeat it 5 times.
- Recall and repeat this mantra throughout the day.
- Harness positive energy via 15 - 20 minutes of meditation.
- Visualize the life you desire.

 **What song are you most glad exists?**

DAILY POSITIVITY

Today is:

I Woke Up At:

Month	1	2	3	4	5	6	7	8	9	10	11	12	Year
	Jan	Feb	Mar	Apr	May	Jun	Jul	Aug	Sep	Oct	Nov	Dec	

TODAY'S GOAL

THREE THINGS I'M GRATEFUL

THREE ACTS OF KINDNESS

TASKS

○ ○ ○ ○ ○ ○ ○ ○ ○ ○ ○ ○ ○ ○ ○ ○ ○ ○

TODAY'S CHALLENGES

THE BEST THING ABOUT TODAY

GOLDEN OPPORTUNITIES

NOTES

LIST OF THINGS
I AM THANKFUL FOR THIS WEEK

WEEK

MONDAY

TUESDAY

WEDNESDAY

THURSDAY

FRIDAY

SATURDAY

SUNDAY

WEEKLY REVIEW

WEEK

MONDAY

TUESDAY

WEDNESDAY

THURSDAY

FRIDAY

SATURDAY

SUNDAY

A SUMMARY OF THE WHOLE WEEK

DAY 29

- Select any affirmation and repeat it 5 times.
- Recall and repeat this mantra throughout the day.
- Harness positive energy via 15 - 20 minutes of meditation.
- Visualize the life you desire.

 What was your favorite birthday like? How can you make tomorrow more like that day?

DAILY POSITIVITY

Today is: I Woke Up At:

Month	1	2	3	4	5	6	7	8	9	10	11	12	Year
	Jan	Feb	Mar	Apr	May	Jun	Jul	Aug	Sep	Oct	Nov	Dec	

TODAY'S GOAL

THREE THINGS I'M GRATEFUL

THREE ACTS OF KINDNESS

TASKS

- ○
- ○
- ○
- ○
- ○
- ○
- ○
- ○
- ○
- ○
- ○
- ○
- ○
- ○
- ○
- ○
- ○

TODAY'S CHALLENGES

THE BEST THING ABOUT TODAY

GOLDEN OPPORTUNITIES

NOTES

DAY 30

- Select any affirmation and repeat it 5 times.
- Recall and repeat this mantra throughout the day.
- Harness positive energy via 15 - 20 minutes of meditation.
- Visualize the life you desire.

 What 5 compliments would you want someone to give you?

DAILY POSITIVITY

Today is: I Woke Up At:

Month 1   2   3   4   5   6   7   8   9   10   11   12   Year
       Jan Feb Mar Apr May Jun Jul Aug Sep Oct Nov Dec

TODAY'S GOAL	THREE THINGS I'M GRATEFUL	THREE ACTS OF KINDNESS

TASKS

○
○
○
○
○
○
○
○
○
○
○
○
○
○
○
○
○

TODAY'S CHALLENGES	THE BEST THING ABOUT TODAY
GOLDEN OPPORTUNITIES	NOTES

BONUS-DAY 31

- Select any affirmation and repeat it 5 times.
- Recall and repeat this mantra throughout the day.
- Harness positive energy via 15 - 20 minutes of meditation.
- Visualize the life you desire.

 List 30 things you are most grateful for today.

DAILY POSITIVITY

Today is:

I Woke Up At:

Month	1	2	3	4	5	6	7	8	9	10	11	12	Year
	Jan	Feb	Mar	Apr	May	Jun	Jul	Aug	Sep	Oct	Nov	Dec	

TODAY'S GOAL

THREE THINGS I'M GRATEFUL

THREE ACTS OF KINDNESS

TASKS

- ○
- ○
- ○
- ○
- ○
- ○
- ○
- ○
- ○
- ○
- ○
- ○
- ○
- ○
- ○
- ○
- ○
- ○

TODAY'S CHALLENGES

THE BEST THING ABOUT TODAY

GOLDEN OPPORTUNITIES

NOTES

NOTES

"Let us be grateful to people who makes us happy, they are the charming gardener who make our soul blossom."

MARCEL PROUST

HAPPINESS & JOY DAILY AFFIRMATIONS

LOVE & RELATIONSHIP DAILY AFFIRMATIONS

MY LIFE IS FULL OF *Love* AND *Romance*

I GIVE AND ACCEPT *Love* FREELY, EASILY, AND JOYFULLY

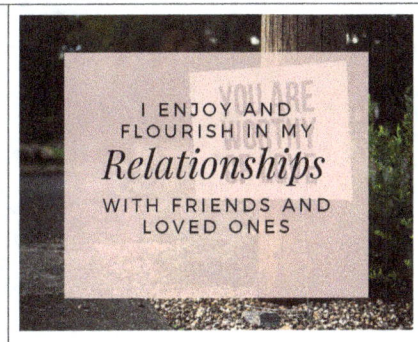

I ENJOY AND FLOURISH IN MY *Relationships* WITH FRIENDS AND LOVED ONES

I FIND *love* EVERYWHERE I GO, AND I RETURN IT IN KIND

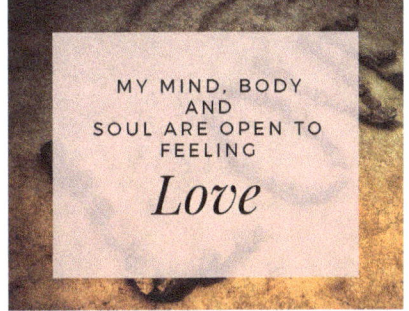

MY MIND, BODY AND SOUL ARE OPEN TO FEELING *Love*

MY *Relationships* ARE HEALTHY, FULFILLING AND IN HARMONY WITH THE HIGHEST GOOD

MY LIFE IS FULL OF *love* AND REWARDING RELATIONSHIPS

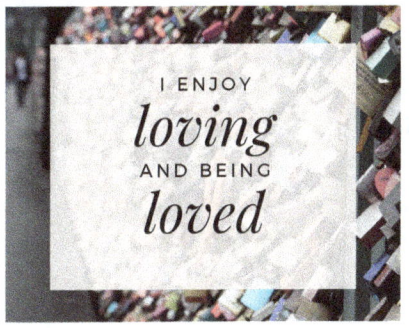

I ENJOY *loving* AND BEING *loved*

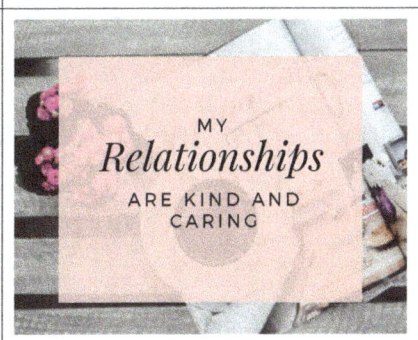

MY *Relationships* ARE KIND AND CARING

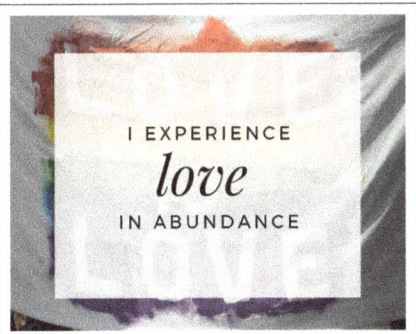

I EXPERIENCE *love* IN ABUNDANCE

I ACCEPT *love* FULLY IN ALL RELATIONSHIPS

I BUILD REWARDING *Relationships* EVERYWHERE I GO

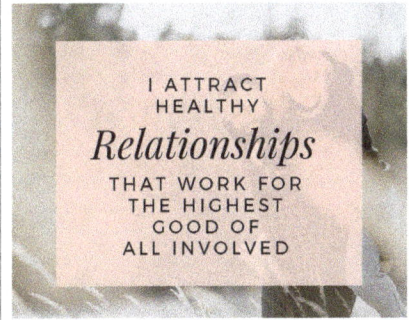

I ATTRACT HEALTHY *Relationships* THAT WORK FOR THE HIGHEST GOOD OF ALL INVOLVED

I ACCEPT PERFECT, DIVINE *love* NOW AND AT ALL TIMES

I AM *Loved*

MONEY & WEALTH DAILY AFFIRMATIONS

SELF LOVE DAILY AFFIRMATIONS

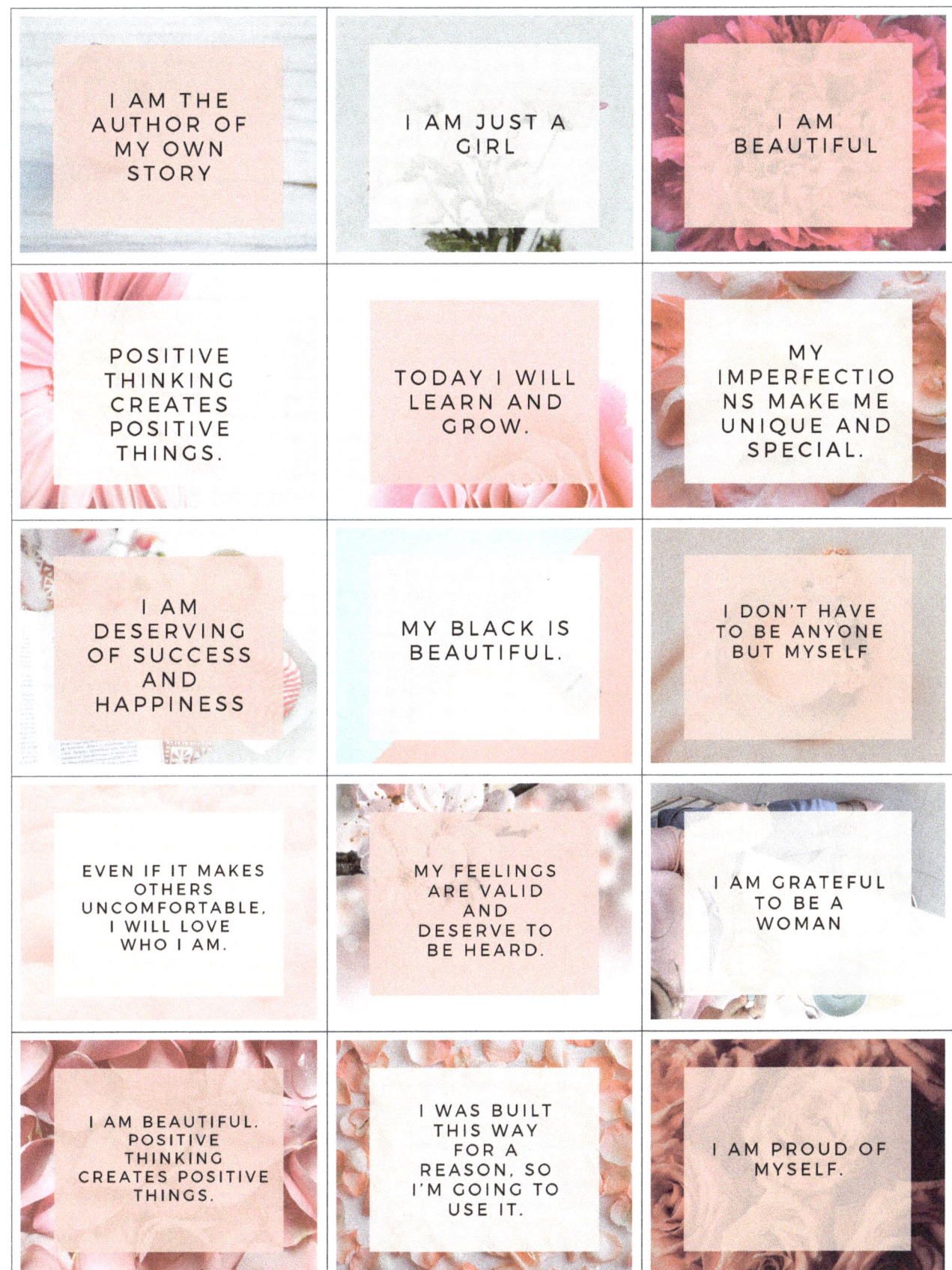

I AM THE AUTHOR OF MY OWN STORY	I AM JUST A GIRL	I AM BEAUTIFUL
POSITIVE THINKING CREATES POSITIVE THINGS.	TODAY I WILL LEARN AND GROW.	MY IMPERFECTIONS MAKE ME UNIQUE AND SPECIAL.
I AM DESERVING OF SUCCESS AND HAPPINESS	MY BLACK IS BEAUTIFUL.	I DON'T HAVE TO BE ANYONE BUT MYSELF
EVEN IF IT MAKES OTHERS UNCOMFORTABLE, I WILL LOVE WHO I AM.	MY FEELINGS ARE VALID AND DESERVE TO BE HEARD.	I AM GRATEFUL TO BE A WOMAN
I AM BEAUTIFUL. POSITIVE THINKING CREATES POSITIVE THINGS.	I WAS BUILT THIS WAY FOR A REASON, SO I'M GOING TO USE IT.	I AM PROUD OF MYSELF.

www.ingramcontent.com/pod-product-compliance
Lightning Source LLC
Chambersburg PA
CBHW081235080526
44587CB00022B/3946